AL–

THE PATH TO PERFECTION

SHAYKH ABDUL RAHEEM LIMBADA

HĀFIZAHULLĀH

Tafseer-Raheemi Publications 2018
info@tafseer-raheemi.com

Al-Qur'ān: The Path to Perfection
1st Edition: Sha'bān 1439 / May 2018
ISBN: 978-1-912301-09-6

Author	Shaykh Abdul Raheem Limbādā [*Hāfizahullāh*] (www.tafseer-raheemi.com)
Editing	Maulānā Omer Anwar
Cover Design	Shaykh Ahmed *ibn* Maulānā Mohammed Patel
Typesetting	Belal Isakjee
Printed by	Mega Printers, Turkey

Available to purchase from www.tafseer-raheemi.com/shop

CONTENTS

PREFACE

بِسْمِ اللهِ الرَّحْمٰنِ الرَّحِيْمِ

نحمده ونصلى على رسوله الكريم. اما بعد.

The Qur'ān is the last and final book of Allāh ﷻ. It is a huge treasure for Muslims, a priceless gem. However, it is probably the book which Muslims have neglected the most.

People read all manner of texts, from novels, to comics, to magazines, newspapers, and journals. However, when it comes to the Qur'ān, they feel heavy hearted.

Hadhrat Maulānā Fazlur Rahmān Ganjmurādabādī رحمه الله was asked: "I enjoy reading other things, but when it comes to the Qur'ān, I struggle to read even a few pages." He replied, "This is because you are distanced from the Qur'ān. When you come close, *Inshā-Allāh*, this feeling will go away." Closeness is achieved by being attached to the Qur'ān.

The *Salaf as-Ṣāliḥīn* loved the Qur'ān so much that they couldn't get enough of its recital. They became *Ahlullāh* by becoming *Ahlul Qur'ān* first. The *Hadīth* states:

ان الله أهلي من الناس قالو امن هم يا رسول الله قال

" اهل القران هم أهل الله وخاصته وأولياؤه "

"Indeed Allāh has close ones among the people. 'Who are they, Ya *Rasūlallāh*?' He was asked. He replied, 'The people of the Qur'ān. They are the close ones to Allāh, and His special ones, and His friends.'"

This small booklet in your hands is the transcription of a talk I had delivered. It was transcribed by some of my family members, which I then edited. I was going to share it on social media, however, my dearest friend Maulana Belal Isakjee suggested that we should make a small booklet out of it in order to benefit a wider audience. May Allāh ﷻ reward him for his *muhabbat* and beautiful suggestion.

May Allāh ﷻ make this booklet beneficial for all of us and be pleased with us. *Āmīn*

(*Shaykh*) Abdul Raheem Limbādā (*Hāfizahullāh*)
15 Sha'bān 1439
Tuesday 1st May 2018

INTRODUCTION

الحمد لله نحمده ونستعينه ونستغفره ونؤمن به ونتوكل عليه ، ونعوذ بالله من شرور انفسنا ومن سيأت اعمالنا ، من يهده الله فلا مضل له ، ومن يضلله فلا هادى له ، ونشهد ان لا اله الا الله وحده لا شريك له ، ونشهد ان سيدنا ومولانا محمدا عبده ورسوله ، صلى الله تعالى عليه وعلى آله وصحبه وبارك وسلم تسليم كثيرا كثيرا ، اما بعد : فأعوذ بالله من الشيطان الرجيم ، بسم الله الرحمن الرحيم۔

اِنَّ هٰذَا الْقُرْاٰنَ يَهْدِيْ لِلَّتِيْ هِيَ اَقْوَمُ وَيُبَشِّرُ الْمُؤْمِنِيْنَ الَّذِيْنَ يَعْمَلُوْنَ الصّٰلِحٰتِ
اَنَّ لَهُمْ اَجْرًا كَبِيْرًا ○ وَاَنَّ الَّذِيْنَ لَا يُؤْمِنُوْنَ بِالْاٰخِرَةِ اَعْتَدْنَا لَهُمْ عَذَابًا اَلِيْمًا ○

"Surely this Qur'ān leads to a path that is straight, and it conveys good news to the believers who do good deeds that they shall have a great reward. And that We have prepared a painful punishment for those who do not believe in the hereafter." [1]

To begin with, we must firstly understand three details:

[1] The Qur'ān is perfect.

---

[1] Qur'ān 17:9-10.

[2] The qualities that constitute a perfect human being and how this perfection can be defined.

[3] The method by which the Qur'ān can make us into perfect human beings.

THE QUR'ĀN IS PERFECT

The Qur'ān begins:

الم ○

Allāh ﷻ knows best what He means by these letters.

ذٰلِكَ الْكِتٰبُ ○

This is the book. *Al-Kitāb al-Kāmil*, i.e. the Complete Book. In other words, this book being revealed to you is 'The Complete Book' and should be classified so, as no other book is as complete. It is the only book worthy of being referred to as 'The Book'.

لَا رَيْبَ فِيْهِ ○

There is no doubt or confusion in this book's divine origin. It is definitely from Allāh ﷻ.

هُدًى لِّلْمُتَّقِينَ ○

It provides guidance for those who have fear of God in their hearts, who are aware of God, and who are constantly conscious of the fact that God exists and that He is aware of everything. Even if you do not believe in Islam, but you have this awareness of God in your heart, then the Qur'ān will guide you. This understanding and awareness is needed to understand His Book.

SOME OBJECTIONS CLARIFIED

Some people may try to create doubts and say, "We don't believe that this is the book of God. There are some contradictions in it." The reason that people find contradictions in the Qur'ān is that they don't look at it with an open mind and a clear heart. If they were to look at it with an open mind and a clear heart, they would see the clarity, the openness, and the purity of the Holy Qur'ān.

If a person is afflicted by jaundice, his own complexion becomes yellow and everything he sees seems yellow to him. Even most white things appear yellow to him. Only when this illness is gone is he able to see things properly again. But the healthy person can see everything properly.

Allāh ﷻ is alluding that you must open your mind and clear your heart, and *then* read the Qur'ān. Then you will be able to see and appreciate its clarity and completeness.

Some people declare there is abrogation in the Qur'ān. In preparation for this talk, I researched various forums and websites across the internet. Many results came up and some objections concerning the abrogation came up as well. They cry that why would Allāh ﷻ abrogate something? Did He not know beforehand that He would have to change His commands? If He knew it, then He should have given the second command in the first place. If He didn't, then He lacks knowledge, which means He cannot be God.

However, a few points should be kept in mind. Firstly, people who raise this objection try to portray it as if the entire Qur'ān is filled with abrogation. Conversely, if you actually look, there are maybe half a dozen or so occurrences of abrogation in the entire Qur'ān such as the changing of the *Qiblah*, the punishment for *zinā*, and the order of *iddat* for a widow. Otherwise all of the orders like *ṣalāh*, fasting, etc. remained as they were.

Secondly, there is no abrogation with regard to the *Akhbār*, i.e. the news or information that Allāh ﷻ gives. It is only the *Aḥkām*, i.e. the instructions, which are on occasion changed. Do this for now. Then He changes the command for reasons known best to Him.

For example, in regards to the *Qiblah*, Allāh ﷻ states that facing east or west is not important. Rather what *is* important is that you do whatever Allāh ﷻ instructs you. Allāh's ﷻ order is what matters. We submit ourselves to Allāh's ﷻ orders and His Divine Will. The reason for facing Baitul Maqdis was to bring Ahlul-Kitab closer. However, when they remained stubborn Allāh ﷻ changed the direction of *Qiblah* to the Ka'ba after 17 months. It's like a doctor who prescribes a medicine and then changes the dose or the medicine altogether as and when needed. So there is no harm in abrogation. Moreover, there is also abrogation in the Bible and Torah so this is not a valid objection upon the Qur'ān.

At times its opponents try to claim it contains contradictions. Yet this is only because they look at the translation and not the deeper meaning of those *Āyāt*. If you read the *tafsīr*, you see that there is no contradiction in the Qur'ān. The *Mufassirīn* such as Imam Qurtubī, Imam Ibn Kathīr, and Imam Fakhruddīn Rāzī رحمهم الله, and recent *Mufassirīn* such as Mufti Muhammad Shafī Sahib, Maulānā Idrīs Khāndelwī Sahib, and Maulānā Ashraf Ali Thanvī رحمهم الله have gone to great lengths to explain the Qur'ān and clear any doubts or contradictions that may arise in one's mind.

For example, the Qur'ān says in *Sūrah Al-Muzzammil*, 'Lord of the East and the West'. Yet, in Sūrah *Ar-Raḥmān*, Allāh ﷻ states 'Lord of the two Easts and the two Wests', while in Sūrah *As-Sāffāt* He ﷻ states 'Lord of all the Easts and all the Wests'. There seems to be a contradiction between these verses. However, deeper insight elaborates that the singular word is used as a generalisation, while the double is used to refer to the farthest and the lowest points of the sun's rising and setting in summer and winter, and the plural is used to convey the different risings and settings which occur daily.

Alhamdulillāh, the Qur'ān is the perfect book. As Muslims, we believe in that. Even the wise men among the non-Muslims also testify to that. I will quote a few paragraphs concerning how non-Muslims felt when they read the Qur'ān.

STATEMENTS OF NON-MUSLIMS REGARDING THEIR FEELINGS ABOUT THE QUR'ĀN

'I started reading the Holy Qur'ān and opened Sūrah *Al-Kawthar*. Small but beautiful sentences pierced into my heart like arrows. Their melodies had a very sweet but everlasting effect in my ears. They were so magical that I repeated the verses unintentionally, and I went on reading them again and again. I felt as if I was drinking from the water of immortality. I was even ready to believe in the true teachings of the Holy Qur'ān just by reading this small Sūrah. However, there were some doubts still in my mind. They were about the Prophethood of the Holy Prophet ﷺ, the position of women in Islam, and issues of the lawful and unlawful, which that pious man removed in a very reasonable and philosophical manner.

In fact, I had found the truth, and unknowingly I pronounced the *Kalimah-e-Tawḥīd*. I was so happy that I could not express my feelings in words.' – *Dr Abdur Rahman Barker*

'The Qur'ān was written [revealed] 1400 years ago. Nothing has changed since then, not even a single full stop. Yet it contains the knowledge of the present moment, science, and the future. It is just a miracle how a book [revealed] in primitive days contains all the events of today and also events of the future which we cannot understand as yet. Islam is not just a religion, but a way of life. So this part of Islam appealed the most to me.' – *Brother Dawood [A revert].*

He goes on to say that reading the Qur'ān and *ḥadīth* were the main things that attracted him towards Islam.

'As a Catholic, I had studied widely and passed the main exams in Catholic theology. The power of Jesus was obvious from the Gospels and the Bible had evidence that his life was predestined. I longed to meet him in the Heavens. There is a line from the first chapter of St. John about Jesus: 'The light shone in the darkness, and the darkness did not understand it.' I started to wonder why my understanding of Jesus was different to what I was being taught in the churches. I never, at that time, read the Qur'ān. Discovering the Qur'ān was a bit like being in a big, old house and going from room to room. The rooms were small and dark, but in each room there were little, interesting things, never enough to satisfy. So I went on to the next room, and then the next room. Suddenly I opened a door and there is a vast, white light that dazzled me. It is impossible to describe the power of the Holy Qur'ān unless you have been deprived of it beforehand. This is because it is the direct word of Allāh ﷻ. It is so obvious. But I shut my eyes because it is too much for me. I find myself opening my eyes a little bit and daring to take in something of its power. But I am only a beginner, and will never be more than that. I can only ask for Allāh's ﷻ Mercy and Compassion to allow me to understand according to my limitations. But one drop of its knowledge is worth more than all of the other books.' – *Amina (Ann) Coxon from London.*

These are testimonies from some people who were not yet Muslims. They read the Qur'ān, were attracted to Islam, and accepted Islam. So *Alhamdulillāh*, the Qur'ān is the perfect book. If you read it with an open mind, it will open up the way for you.

Hadhrat Maulānā Aḥmed Ạlī Lāhorī رحمه الله used to say, 'The *Ulamā* should teach the Qur'ān and have lessons and discourses on it, because the example of the Qur'ān is like that of flowing water. It makes its own way. The Qur'ān flows and makes its own way inside hearts and you don't need to make way for it.'

Having understood that the Qur'ān is a perfect book, our second task here is to now define the qualities that constitute a perfect human being and who can be regarded as such.

WHO IS THE PERFECT HUMAN BEING ?

Can we define the perfect person as one who is strong, smart, rich, or well educated? Even a person with each and every one of these qualities can have many flaws. Such people may be perfect in their fields, but when we look at other aspects such as their character, manners, empathy, worship, fear of Allāh ﷻ, fulfilling the rights of Allāh ﷻ and the rights of the creation of Allāh ﷻ etc., they might fall well below expectations. Therefore, I would say instead that the perfect human being is the one with the best conduct and thus a perfect heart – i.e. a heart that has the most taqwā, fear, and awareness of Allāh ﷻ.

The most perfect human being, the one with the best conduct and most perfect heart was none but *Rasūlullāh* ﷺ. He was the most kind, most humble, most generous, most pious, and most beloved to Allāh ﷻ. One *ḥadīth* says that Allāh ﷻ looked at the hearts of the human beings to be created until the Day of *Qiyāmah* and saw that the best heart was that of Muḥammad ﷺ, so He chose him to be the leader of mankind.

Maybe this is why Allāh ﷻ made him '*Uswā-e-Ḥasanah*', the most beautiful role model, and instructed us to look up to him, follow in his footsteps, adapt his lifestyle, and sacrifice everything in his love. The more we resemble him the closer we will be to Allāh ﷻ.

When Sayyidatunā Ā'isha رضي الله عنها was asked about the *akhlāq* of *Rasūlullāh* ﷺ, she replied, 'His characteristics were the Qur'ān [i.e. he was the practical Qur'ān and whatever Allāh ﷻ has instructed in the Qur'ān, he would practice upon it]'.

This brings us to the question: how can we gain such perfection through the Qur'ān? The answer is that it can be achieved by implementing the following points:

[1] Respect the Qur'ān.
[2] Recite the Qur'ān.
[3] Memorise the Qur'ān.
[4] Understand the Qur'ān.
[5] Practice upon the Qur'ān.

RESPECT THE QUR'ĀN

It is of utmost importance that we show respect to the Qur'ān. Sadly, these days, many people treat the Qur'ān like a regular book. Some put it on the floor, while others claim that you don't need to have *wudhū* to touch the Qur'ān. You can touch it without *wudhū*.

MAS'ALA OF *WUDHŪ* FOR TOUCHING THE QUR'ĀN

While we are discussing this, allow me to explain that it is *wājib* to have *wudhū* to touch the Qur'ān. There is a consensus upon this among the four Imams, Imam *Abū* Hanīfāh, Imam Mālik, Imam Shāfi'ī, and Imam Ahmad ﷺ. In fact, Imam Mālik and Imam Shāfi'ī say that if the reciter's *Wudhū* breaks during recitation, it is not permissible to even turn the pages of the Qur'ān with a pencil or a piece of cloth. He should immediately perform *wudhū* and then continue with the recitation. Imam *Abū* Hanīfāh and Imam Ahmad, however, allow turning the pages of the Qur'ān with a pencil or something similar. This shows how important it is to have *Wudhū* when touching the Qur'ān.

Some people object to this and ask for a *ḥadīth* as proof. I ask when providing evidence, what comes first? Qur'ān or *ḥadīth*? First, we should take *dalīl* from Qur'ān and *then* from *ḥadīth*.

Allāh ﷻ says in Sūrah Wāqi'ah:

فَلَآ اُقْسِمُ بِمَوٰقِعِ النُّجُوْمِ ○ وَاِنَّهٗ لَقَسَمٌ لَّوْ تَعْلَمُوْنَ عَظِيْمٌ ○
اِنَّهٗ لَقُرْاٰنٌ كَرِيْمٌ ○ فِيْ كِتٰبٍ مَّكْنُوْنٍ ○ لَّا يَمَسُّهٗٓ اِلَّا الْمُطَهَّرُوْنَ ○

'I swear by the falling of the stars. And it is a great oath, if only you knew. Most surely, this is a noble Qur'ān. In a book

that is protected. None shall touch it save the purified ones.
A revelation by the Lord of the worlds.' [2]

The above verse is not merely informing: it is an order. None should touch the Qur'ān unless they are pure, clean, and *Pāk*. Dr Muhsin Khan has twisted the translation of these verses by inserting his own interpretation in brackets. He writes: 'Which (that book with Allāh ﷻ) none can touch but the purified (i.e. the angels)'. He failed to understand that reference is not towards '*fī kitābim maknūn*', but rather the indication is towards '*Qur'ānun Karīm*'. He did not realise that in the Arabic language words of information can be used for a command. This is why the verse is translated as 'None shall / should touch it.'

Let us look to the *Ṣaḥābah* ﷺ for the *tafsīr* of this *āyah*, as they were the first narrators of the Qur'ān and understood it better than anyone else. Sa'īd ibn Manṣūr, Ibn Abī Shaybah, Ibn al-Mundhir, and Ḥākim (who classifies the narration as *Ṣaḥīḥ*) all narrate from Ạbdur Raḥmān ibn Zayd ﷺ that we were once with Salmān Fārsī ﷺ and he went for *istinjā* (to relieve himself). When he returned, we asked him if he could perform *wudhū* so that we could sit down with him and ask a few questions about the Qur'ān. He replied, 'Ask me any

[2] Qur'ān 56:75-79. Translation by Ahmed Shākir.

question you want because I am not going to touch the Qur'ān. *Wudhū* is only needed when you want to touch the Qur'ān. Then he recited the *āyah*:

لَّا يَمَسُّهُۥٓ إِلَّا ٱلْمُطَهَّرُونَ ○

. . . Which means that the Qur'ān should not be touched without *wudhū*.'

This *tafsīr* is taken by all four Imams and majority of the *Mufassirīn*.

In *Al-Fiqh al-Islāmī wa Adillatuhū*, Dr Wahaba az-Zuhaili writes that if you have the minor impurity, three things are not allowed:

[1] Performing *ṣalāh* and anything like *ṣalāh*. For example, *sajdah* of *tilāwah*, *sajdah* of *shukr* and *ṣalātul janāzah*. This is because *Rasūlullāh* ﷺ mentioned this in a *ḥadīth*: '*Ṣalāh* is not accepted without *ṭuhūr*' [3]

[2] *Ṭawāf* of *Baytullāh Sharīf*. (One *ḥadīth* says '*Ṭawāf* of *Baytullāh* is *ṣalāh*, except that Allāh ﷻ has allowed us to talk during *ṭawāf*).

[3] Tirmīdhī.

[3] Touching the *Musḥaf* or part of it because of the aforementioned *āyah* and because of the *ḥadīth:*

لا يمس القران الا طاهر.

Which is narrated by Imam Abū Dāwūd, Imam Nasa'ī, and Imam Mālik in his Muwatta (mursal) on the authority Amr ibn Ḥazm, and by Dāraqutnī. It is also narrated by Baihaqī from Ạbdullāh ibn Ụmar رضي الله عنه and by Tabrānī from Ụthmān ibn Abul Ạāṣ رضي الله عنه. The narration translates as, 'None should touch the Qur'ān except a person with *ṭahārah'.* And a further logical proof would be that touching without *wudhū* is against *tạẓīmul* Qur'ān (honouring the Qur'ān). In fact, it comes in a *ḥadīth* narrated by Imam Ṭaḥāwī that once *Rasūlullāh* ﷺ was performing *wudhū* and a *Ṣaḥābī* passed by and said *salām. Rasūlullāh* ﷺ remained quiet and continued performing *wudhū*. When he completed the *wudhū*, he replied to the *salām* and explained to the *Ṣaḥābī* that he delayed returning the *salām* because 'I disliked taking the name of Allāh ﷻ without *wudhū.*'

Rasūlullāh ﷺ had so much respect for the name of Allāh ﷻ, that he did not like to say 'As-Salām' without *wudhū*. Qur'ān is the word of Allāh ﷻ. How can one touch it without *wudhū*?

Another question that arises here due to the fact that today we have the Qur'ān in many other forms besides the *musḥaf* (i.e. in smartphones, iPads, laptops, etc.) When we are NOT opening the Qur'ān in them can we touch them without *wudhū*? The answer is yes, because the gadget itself is like any other book of *Tafsīr*, *Ḥadīth*, or *Fiqh* which contain verses of the Qur'ān but also other material besides them as well. Similarly, there are other materials in these gadgets like various files, books of *Ḥadīth*, etc.

However, when opening the Qur'ān and scrolling the pages, you should not touch the letters of the Qur'ān without *wudhū*. If one does not have *wudhū*, they can use the stylus pen to scroll up and down. It is always best to try to read with *wudhū*, but when that is not possible, then this would be allowed. If one is reciting on a computer he may scroll through the pages with a mouse. Many workers do that in the office at lunch time during Ramadhān.

LOOKING IN THE MUSḤAF DURING *SALĀH*.

Some people put the Qur'ān on the floor. Others look inside and recite it while performing *ṣalāh*, especially during *Tarāwīh* behind the imām. When they go into *Rukū*, they put it under their armpit; when they go into *sajdah*, they put it on the floor. What is the need to read from musḥaf during *ṣalāh*? In fact, it is prohibited. Allāh ﷻ says:

وَاِذَا قُرِئَ الْقُرْاٰنُ فَاسْتَمِعُوْا لَهٗ وَاَنْصِتُوْا لَعَلَّكُمْ تُرْحَمُوْنَ ○

And when the Qur'ān is recited, listen attentively, and remain silent so that you may be shown mercy' [4]

Your focus should be on Allāh ﷻ, not on trying to read yourself. You should focus on the imām's recitation and concentrate. Placing the *mushaf* under the armpit or on the floor is contrary to the reverence of the Qur'ān.

Shaykh Ạbdul Ạzīz ibn Bāz رحمه الله was once asked about this and he stated that it is against the *adab* (propriety) of the Qur'ān. The Qur'ān should be placed on a high place. In fact, we are taught to respect the books of the other religions as well, because the followers of those religions respect their books.

He went on to quote a *ḥadīth* in which the Jews of Madīnah Munawwara came to *Rasūlullāh* ﷺ to ask a *mas'ala*. *Rasūlullāh* ﷺ told them to bring the Torah and search for the *mas'ala* in there. When they brought it, *Rasūlullāh* ﷺ asked someone to bring a chair and then placed the Torah on the chair rather than on the floor.

Another thing to mention here is that in some public places like hospitals, multi-faith prayer rooms, etc., we find books of other religions. Some *jāhil* people tear off some pages or scribble graffiti on them. This is wrong. The followers of those

---

[4] Qur'ān 7:204.

religions revere their books and we should not hurt anyone's feelings.

To summarise, if we want the Qur'ān to transform us into perfect human beings, we must, first of all, show some respect to the Qur'ān.

There are many other etiquettes of reciting the Qur'ān and many books have been written on this subject. Imam Nawawī ؒ has written 'At-Tibyān fī Ādābi Ḥamalat al-Qur'ān' and Hadhrat Shaykh Zakariyyā ؒ has written the renowned 'Fazāil-e-Qur'ān'.

Some of the ādāb (etiquettes) mentioned therein include making wudhū before reciting, keeping the Qur'ān on an elevated place such as a pillow or rehal, being focused, applying itr (perfume), facing the Qiblah, reading with tajwīd and tartīl, reading with fear and awareness of Allāh ﷻ, and reading with a soft melodious tone, etc.

Only when we follow these ādāb will we be able to absorb the benefits of the Qur'ān.

RECITING THE QUR'ĀN

The more one recites the Qur'ān, the better it is for him. Rasūlullāh ﷺ has said that the heart rusts just as metal rusts when continuously exposed to water. When our hearts are continuously exposed to fitnah, they likewise become rusted. Rasūlullāh ﷺ has mentioned two medicines for curing and cleansing our hearts: to remember death abundantly and to recite the Qur'ān.

AN OBJECTION AND ITS ANSWER

Some people posit an objection, in that there is no point in the recitation of the Qur'ān when the reader does not understand it. This is a *waswasa*, a misguidance which Shayṭān whispers in one's mind. They make this objection because they view the Qur'ān as a book, to be categorised with other books, where the benefits are exclusive to those that understand the languages they are written in. For example, a Spanish or French book is of no use to a reader that exclusively understands English.

However, this is not the case with the Qur'ān. The Qur'ān is not like other books. It is the book of Allāh ﷻ. For every letter read, Allāh ﷻ rewards the reader with ten *ḥasanāt*, which are recorded in your register of good deeds. For *Alif-Laam-Meem*, the reader is rewarded with at least 30 good deeds; for *Bismillāh-hir-Rahman-nir-Raheem*, 190 good deeds; for *Surah Ikhlāṣ*, 990 good deeds; and for *Surah Yāsīn*, 30,000 good deeds. The benefits of a Qur'anic recitation reach far beyond the understanding of the reader.

One *Ḥadīth* states that *tilāwah* brings *Noor* for the reciter. Another *Ḥadīth* declares the reciters as *Ahl-Allāh*, i.e. the special people of Allāh ﷻ. These are not exclusive benefits for Arabic speakers.

Those that cannot pronounce the letters correctly should go to learn from someone that can help them with the *Noorani Qaidah*, as should New Muslims and reverts. Do not exclusively focus on understanding the meaning. The importance of understanding the Qur'an is not in doubt here, and I will look into the matter later. However, the recitation of the Qur'ān is also a right that the Qur'ān has upon us, and should be fulfilled.

If the Qur'ān is not recited, it will hold us to account on the Day of Judgement and we will have to answer to Allāh ﷻ. The Qur'ān will say, 'What type of a Muslim were they when you sent me to them and they never read me, never opened me?' May Allāh ﷻ protect us.

Imām Abū Ḥanīfah رحمه الله said that there are two categories of Muslims: The *Ḥāfiẓ* and the non-*Ḥāfiẓ*. According to the Imām رحمه الله, the *Ḥāfiẓ* should at the very least complete one *khatam* of the Qur'ān every 40 days. However, it is better for him to recite 3 *juz* every day and complete one *khatam* every ten days, and better still to read one *manzil* a day and complete a *khatam* every week. As For the non-*Ḥāfiẓ*, it is necessary to complete two *khatam's* a year. This is easily done with a consistent routine, and therefore every Muslim should endeavour to do so.

OUR AKĀBIR'S PRACTICES

Some *shuyūkh* would complete a *khatam* every single day. Imam Shāfi'ī رحمه الله was a very zealous reciter and was known to increase his *tilāwah* in Ramadhān so much so that he would complete 60 *khatam's*. The same is narrated about Imam Abū Ḥanīfah رحمه الله and many other *Salaf* of that era.

During Ramadhan, Imam Bukhārī رحمه الله would recite 10 *juz* in *Nawāfil* at night and complete one *khatam* every day, thus completing 40 *khatam's* every Ramadhān (one every day, plus one every three nights in nawāfil). He used to say that when the Qur'ān is completed, duās are readily accepted by Allāh ﷻ.

In one narration, *Rasūlullāh* ﷺ says that when someone completes a recital of the Qur'ān, 60,000 angels make duā of *raḥmah* (Mercy) and *maghfirah* (Forgiveness) for that person.

Sayyidunā Ụthmān Ghanī, Saeed Ibn Jubair, Tamīm Dārī, and Imam Abū Ḥanīfah رحمه الله are all reported to have recited the whole Qur'ān in one *rak'ạh*. Imam Abū Ḥanīfah رحمه الله did this inside the Ka'ba Sharīf.

They had a special love for the Qur'ān. When they recited it, it was as if they had entered another world and became completely oblivious to their surroundings. *Sayyidunā* Ụthmān Ghanī رضي الله عنه would say:

لو ان قلوبنا طهرت ما شبعنا من كلام ربنا.

'If our hearts were cleansed we would never be satiated with the speech of our Rabb.'

Rasūlullāh ﷺ said that Allāh ﷻ raises the ranks of many people through the Qur'ān and lowers many people through the Qur'ān as well. This encompasses *tilāwah* as well.

May Allāh ﷻ make us amongst the ones whose ranks are raised by the Qur'ān. *Āmīn.*

MEMORISING THE QUR'ĀN

It is *farḍh* upon every Muslim to memorise so much of the Qur'ān that the obligatory *rukn* of *ṣalāh* can be fulfilled. Otherwise, without *tilāwah*, *ṣalāh* will not be valid.

Thereafter, every Muslim should memorise as much of the Qur'ān as they can. *Rasūlullāh* ﷺ said that the heart in which there is no Qur'ān, is like an empty, deserted, and derelict house. If we want our heart to be furnished with the mercy of Allāh ﷻ, we should make an effort to memorise His Qur'ān.

If one succeeds in memorising the whole Qur'ān and becomes a Ḥāfiẓ, then *Subḥān-Allāh*! There are many glad tidings for them.

In one *Ḥadīth* it is narrated, 'Whoever recites the Qur'ān and commits it to his memory, and then takes its halāl as halāl and it's harām as harām, Allāh ﷻ will admit him in Jannah and accept his intercession for ten such persons of his family who were destined for Jahannam.'

In another *Ḥadīth* it is stated, 'The one who is an expert of the Qur'ān will be resurrected on the day of judgement among those angels who are the envoys, the noble, and the dutiful.' These are the guardians of the *Lawh e Maḥfūẓ*, angels that are extremely pious and honoured in the eyes of Allāh ﷻ. The hāfiz will be resurrected with them, perhaps because they protect the *Lawh e Maḥfūẓ* in the heavens and the Ḥāfiẓ protects the Qur'ān on the Earth.

It is also important to keep the Qur'ān committed to memory throughout one's life. There are grave warnings for those that forget the Qur'ān.

If you become a *pakka* Ḥāfiẓ, it will become easy to recite the Qur'ān while sitting, standing, lying down, walking, driving, working etc. If you look at history, the great scholars and mashāikh were all *Ḥuffāz.* That is why Hadhrat Junaid Baghdādī رحمه الله says 'A person who is not *Ḥāfiẓ* and has not written the *ḥadīth* has nothing to do with this affair of ours (meaning *tasawwuf*)'.

Today, we see on the TV channels that people who are not even *Ḥāfiẓ* of the Qur'ān are giving Fatwas. Dr Zakir Naik is not *Ḥāfiẓ.* He only memorises those *Āyāt* which are pertinent to his arguments. He is not an *Ālim.* He doesn't even know the Arabic language, he relies on translations. So he is not qualified to give verdicts on *fiqhi* issues. Yet he says things like you can touch the Qur'ān without *Wudhū*, three *talāqs* are one, and there is no difference between the *ṣalāh* of men and women. He even claims that *Zakāh* can be given for the running cost of a TV channel. He mistranslates many verses of the Qur'ān. Be very careful in acquiring knowledge from such people.

UNDERSTANDING THE QUR'ĀN

Moving on, *tadabbur* and *tafakkur* when reciting the Qur'ān are highly effective. Allāh ﷻ and His *Rasūl* ﷺ have encouraged us to ponder over the words of Allāh ﷻ. We should try to read the Qur'ān with utmost concentration. If we are able to learn the Arabic language and understand the meaning of the Qur'ān, then we should do so. In this way we will get a lot of enjoyment in *ṣalāh* and in listening to *tilāwah*. If we understand it, and focus on the meanings, it will bring tears to our eyes. It will increase our *ma'rifah* of Allāh ﷻ, resulting in proximity to Allāh ﷻ. Every time we ponder over the meanings, Allāh ﷻ will inspire us with insights into its various sciences.

Sir Marmaduke Pickthall writes in the forward of his translation of the Qur'ān: 'The Qur'ān cannot be translated. That is the belief of the old-fashioned Shaykhs and the view of the present writer. The book is here rendered almost literally and every effort has been made to choose befitting language. But the result is not the Glorious Qur'ān, that inimitable symphony, the very sounds of which move men to tears and ecstasy. It is only an attempt to present the meaning of the Qur'ān - and peradventure something of the charm - in

English. It can never take the place of the Qur'ān in Arabic, nor is it meant to do so.'

The Qur'ān says:

اَفَلَا يَتَدَبَّرُوْنَ الْقُرْاٰنَ اَمْ عَلٰى قُلُوْبٍ اَقْفَالُهَا ۝

'Do they not ponder over the Qur'ān?
Or are there locks on some hearts? [5]

Therefore, we should try to learn Arabic and read tafsīr in Arabic. If this is not possible, then we should try to read tafsīr in our mother tongue. Many good tafsīrs are available in English, e.g. Tafsīr Majidi, Tafsir Mā'riful Qur'ān, Anwārul Bayān, Qur'ān Made Easy.

PRACTICING UPON THE QUR'ĀN

Lastly, we should practice upon the Qur'ān. The Qur'ān does not just teach us *ṣalāh*, *zakāh*, *ṣawm*, and worship. It teaches us *ạqā'id*, *ịbādāt*, akhlāq, *mu'āmalāt*, social life, and much more. We must practice on what we learn.

It is stated in the Hadīth of our mother Ā'isha ﵂ that the akhlāq of *Rasūlullāh* ﷺ was the Qur'ān, i.e he was the walking talking Qur'ān. His whole life revolved around the Qur'ān and its injunctions.

[5] Qur'ān 47:24.

The words وعمل بما فيه are mentioned in many aḥādīth. In one Hadīth: "فاحل حلاله وحرم حرامه" is mentioned. Therefore, we need to practice upon the Qur'ān.

To conclude, I will share with you one quote of Ạbdullāh ibn Mas'ūd ﷺ narrated by Abū Nu'aym in *Ḥilyatul Awliyā*. He says that a person who has been gifted with the Qur'ān, should observe the following things:

[1] Worship at night when others are sleeping.
[2] Fast during the day while people are eating.
[3] Worry about life after death while others are rejoicing.
[4] Cry to Allāh ﷻ while others are laughing.

Rasūlullāh ﷺ has said in one *ḥadīth* that the Qur'ān has been revealed with a sorrowful effect. When you are reading it, cry. If you cannot cry, at least imitate the one who is crying [put on the resemblance of one who is crying].

[5] Hold onto silence when others are idle talking.
[6] Be humble when others are showing arrogance.

He says that it is befitting for a *Ḥāfiẓ* of the Qur'ān to have a habit of crying often, staying in a sorrowful state, being wise, forbearing, a man of knowledge and calm, and an embodiment of peace. He should never be hard-hearted, arrogant, cunning, deceitful, or neglectful. He should never be in a state of *ghaflat* (heedlessness). He must be very careful with the matters of Allāh ﷻ.

Once, *Sayyidunā* Umar ؓ sent a letter to the governors of various cities requesting them to send him a list of all of the *ḥuffāẓ* in their areas so that he could send them a special gift. Abū Mūsā Ash'arī ؓ sent him a list of 300 *ḥuffāẓ* in his area. Umar ؓ was extremely happy and wrote a letter to those *ḥuffāẓ*, the translation of which is below:

This Qur'ān will be a reward for you, and an honour and a treasure, provided you follow it. Make sure that the Qur'ān does not follow you and come after you, because if the Qur'ān comes after someone, then it will hold that person by the scruff of their neck, pin them down and fling them into *Jahannam*. Whosoever follows the Qur'ān, the Qur'ān will pull them towards the Gardens of Firdaus. If it is possible for you, then make sure that the Qur'ān is an intercessor for you and not a claimant against you, because when the Qur'ān intercedes for someone, it takes that person to *Jannah*. And when it makes a claim against someone, then they will have to enter *Jahannam*. Know that the Qur'ān is the fountain of knowledge, the beacon of guidance. It is as fresh as it could be. It has come from *Raḥmān*. It is the most fresh Book of Allāh ﷻ. Allāh ﷻ has opened with it many eyes that were blind, many ears that were deaf, and many hearts that were curtained and veiled. Get up in the night and read the Qur'ān, because when a person gets up at night and thoroughly cleans his mouth with *miswāk* and performs *wudhū* and says *Allāhu Akbar* (i.e. starts *ṣalāh*), an angel comes and puts his mouth on the person's mouth and says: 'Read. Read, for you are good, and goodness has been destined for you.' But if a person doesn't clean his mouth properly, then the angel doesn't do that, but only guards and protects him. Know that the Qur'ān is a treasure, a protector, and goodness preserved. Read the Qur'ān abundantly because *ṣalāh* is *Noor*, *zakāh* an evidence, Patience an illumination, Fasting a shield, and the Qur'ān is either an evidence for you or against you. Respect the Qur'ān; do not degrade it. Whoever honours the Qur'ān, Allāh ﷻ will honour him, and whoever degrades the Qur'ān, Allāh ﷻ will degrade him. Know that whoever memorises, recites and practices upon the Qur'ān, Allāh ﷻ will accept his duā and know that whatever is with Allāh ﷻ is better for those who believe in Allāh ﷻ and put their trust in Allāh ﷻ'. [6]

May Allāh ﷻ give us the *taufique* to understand the value of the Qur'ān, and to respect, recite, memorise, and practice upon the instructions given within the Qur'ān. *Āmīn.*

---

[6] Tuḥfā e Ḥuffāẓ.